Mystery Writers Resource

By Jerry Hooten

ISBN-13: 9781482099799

ISBN-10: 1482099799

Part - I
Covert CCTV

Introduction

What's this book about? My goal is to make it a reference manual for mystery writers to help them with the technical aspect of police work. I had considerable experience in this field and would like to make my services available to any writers that consider themselves "technically challenged".

First of all, most of this experience took place in the 1980's & 90's. Therefore, a lot of the equipment used is dated; however, there are still a lot of the old systems around.

There are a great number of really good articles and books on what "to do" to write a novel. I include some of the "Not to do". We made some boo-boo's and had some equipment failures also.

I'm going to try to stay within the area of my past experiences and use that for the basis of my references. I made different chapters pertaining to different aspects of reference that the writer may want to include in his or her mystery.

The first portion is about covert CCTV equipment and the various applications of that equipment. I've included the techniques I used in the past and those of some of my colleagues as well. We all had our favorite methods and tools to use on the job. You can pick which suits your character best.
When I describe a technique, I'll try to explain why certain things were done to make them more easily understood and how they can be adapted for the writers use.

I am still a great fan of the mystery novel, and so this book is also about the mixture of writing mystery fiction and reality. In my opinion, the closer the two are, the better the fiction is. Reality is hard to change, but fiction is up to the writer. I've had a lot more experience with the reality part of mysteries than the writing of them.

I've had around twenty-five years of experience in law enforcement and security. Some of that experience was on the street, a lot of it was doing electronic surveillance, mostly video.

A lot of mysteries have involvement with some kind of technical equipment. Wire taps, hidden cameras, covert surveillance, hidden microphones, computer hackers, and computer crime, all of the good stuff! Just like with reality!

I am attempting to share some of my experiences from actual cases to assist the mystery writers, to make their writing more realistic. I will try to explain the function of the equipment, how it is used and how it is installed. I will also share some of the bloopers and screw-ups!

There are two other sections in the book, a section on weapons, and one about paper work involved in police work. Nothing can be accomplished in this area without paper!.

Any detective or private eye will eventually encounter an alarm system, and if it's a good one, there will be all of the components of an integrated system, intrusion detection, CCTV, and access control. Along with the security system, you will encounter locks. Door locks, padlocks, window locks and car locks. All of the parts of a good security system are designed to deter, delay and detect. A good security system adds flavor to a good mystery plot.

Hopefully, this handbook will be used as a reference for material you could probably look up on your own, except for the real-life installs! I hope it is entertaining also.

If you want specific help, be sure to visit my website at www.jerryhooten.com. My contact information is there.

Overview

Covert equipment usually covers audio and video surveillance and installations. It is nearly impossible to keep abreast of developments in this fast growing field. A lot of the equipment formerly used for undercover operations is now available for home security use.

Mystery writers often like to include the use of surveillance equipment in their works to add realism to the story. The best way to do this is to not make obvious mistakes in the installation techniques or the equipment itself.

I have included some of the more common pieces of equipment, their use and installation methods. There is all kind of exotic equipment available now, from cameras in pens and eyeglasses to devices that record keystrokes on a computer.

The average law enforcement agency has a limited budget for surveillance equipment so the inclusion of surveillance equipment is usually pretty restricted. Some federal agencies will assist the locals, especially if there is overlapping jurisdiction. Usually, the feds have a bigger budget in this area.

In real life, Technical Investigators install the equipment. Most investigators, detectives, or what have you, do not have the technical ability to install or operate this very complex equipment.

Most of these techs belong to, or are at least aware of NATIA, the National Technical Investigators Association. Quoting from their website, www.natia.org: "The National Technical

Investigators' Association is a non-profit law enforcement educational association. The purpose of NATIA is to further knowledge, develop skills and promote fellowship between those law enforcement and intelligence professionals who support their agencies' and departments' technical surveillance, tactical operations, and forensic activities." Membership in this organization is limited to full-time law enforcement personnel.

NATIA evaluates new equipment and methods and report the results to their members. They invite manufacturers of equipment to their annual national meetings, where they also conduct training forums on new technologies and methods.

The department techs get together at these meetings to exchange ideas and "war stories". Regional meetings are also held on a more frequent basis.

I've tried to put the equipment descriptions and installation methods into a format that the writer can adapt to his story. Methods and equipment will vary from tech to tech. I think most of them would agree that the pieces of equipment I've included are practical for the reasons I've included with the equipment descriptions.

The video equipment I describe is what has been developed using the "chip" cameras and is available on the market. The new cameras are incredibly small, and are easily hidden. They can be installed in a ceiling, a wall, in everyday objects, such as clocks or radios or hidden in clothing.
Once you know how they work and what their limitations are, the only restriction to their use is the scope of your imagination.

CCD Cameras

(Actual cameras)

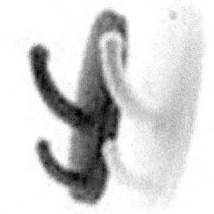

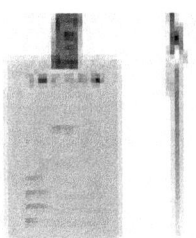

Coat Hook Camera

ID Camera

Rock Camera

The invention of the CCD (Charge Coupled Device) video camera opened a whole new world to the business of surveillance. CMOS (complementary metal oxide semiconductor) cameras are similar and both are used for the new systems. The differences are transparent to most users, so I won't go into the properties here. Prior to them, video cameras were big and bulky, sensitive to light changes and required, comparatively, a lot of electrical current to operate. With the emergence of the CCD's, video surveillance entered a new era.

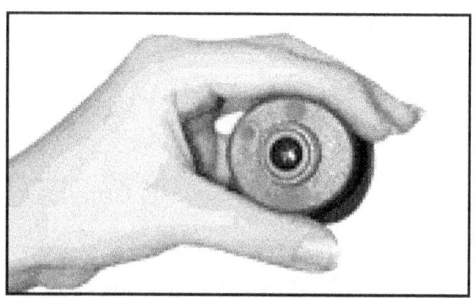

(Complete CCD camera)

(CCD Camera with pinhole lens)

Ah, the good old days! I remember lugging a camera up a ladder to install above a ceiling. The camera, with its six inch long pinhole lens, was over a foot and half in length.

The camera, with a home made mount, had to sit on a ceiling tile. Camera and mount weighed in at about fifteen pounds. The weight had to be supported by using boards laid across the ceiling tile. It kept the whole works from crashing through the ceiling to the floor!

The ceiling tile had to be drilled so that the lens could look through a small hole at the target. Most ceiling tile is about ½" thick. The pinhole lens has an angled end, sort of in a cone configuration. The tip of the cone, which contains the lens, has to be pointed at the target area. In order to do that, the ceiling tile has to be carved by hand to fit. The closer to a vertical shot, the easier it is to cut the tile and the smaller the hole for the lens to look through.

We always tried to keep the angle as near to vertical as possible, to avoid detection. Most ceiling tile has a rough textured surface, so the small hole for the lens was virtually invisible.

The old cameras had to be powered from a 110 volt ac power source, so I would run a zip cord from the camera, down through the wall to an outlet. Zip cord is just a two conductor wire like a lamp cord.

The process for finding the circuit that controlled the camera was to short the outlet and then check circuit breakers to see which one had been popped. The method involved was to use two screwdrivers, sticking them into the outlet, and then

9

touching the shafts together. After the sparks quit flying, it was pretty easy to find which breaker controlled the outlet.

The zip cord was then attached to the outlet at the back side, out of sight. We could either lock out the circuit, or in some cases, bypass it so that the camera would not be inadvertently turned off at the breaker. Procedure at most facilities was for the last person leaving the area would use the breakers to extinguish the lights, sometimes turning off outlets as well.

In some instances, the video recorder was also installed above the ceiling tiles. The recorder was similar to the typical VHS recorders used for home video. These particular units were capable of running in a time lapse mode, recording over a long period of time. The start and stop time could be programmed also to cover the hours in which we were most interested.

The camera would be connected to the recorder with coaxial cable, usually RG-59 or equivalent, a designation for a cable that would give the best performance for a video signal. Video cable has a 75 ohm impedance match for best resolution. The connectors for the cable that couples the camera to the recorder were usually what are known as "BNC". All this was variable, as we were dependent upon time and space and availability. We made up our own cables, cutting them to length and attaching the connectors to each end. Sometimes the only option was to use regular telephone hook-up wire, a four conductor light gauge wire. It was surprising what would work when we were really in a pinch.

The camera and recorder were powered from the same source when they were both above the ceiling tile. If we had the luxury of having a private space to put the recorder, we would generally have a small monitor attached to the recorder also. With the monitor, we could set the time and date on the time/date generator that was incorporated in the recorder. This is the small time and date displayed at the bottom or top of the video. It would have to be set and positioned on the screen for each installation, ensuring that the display didn't cover any area that needed to be viewed. Besides setting the time and date, the position and size of the display could also be adjusted at the recorder.

If a separate area wasn't available, the time and date would be set by carrying the monitor up the ladder and attaching it to the recorder until the time and date was set. Then the monitor would be disconnected.

(Back View of Ouput jacks on Video
Recorder – These are RCA jacks)

Most of the time, the tape would be viewed at a remote location. Sometimes even in a different state. The old tape would be ejected, and a new one inserted at the target site, then the tape would be delivered to the case officer for viewing.

Sometimes the case officer or the tech would do this, but usually we had someone that worked at the site or a local police officer to retrieve the tape and mail it to us.
It is very important that if the tape has evidence of a crime on it that the tabs on the cassette would be removed so that the tape cannot be re-recorded!

The first thing to be done with an evidence tape is to make a working copy of it. The original tape should be labeled and stored in a locked evidence room. Then, copies can be made from the working copy for distribution to whoever needs a copy, or for enhancement or printing of stills, or whatever.

I will never forget a case we had been working on for months. The installation had been difficult, and we had finally videotaped the criminal act in progress! I don't even remember the actual crime, just the circumstances.

The case officer was so proud that we had finally wrapped up the investigation that he just had to show the tape to his team leader and the prosecuting attorney. Using the only copy of the tape we had, he put the tape into the VCR and pushed a button to play the tape for his assembled audience. Wrong Button! He erased the tape and lost the evidence.

Booboos like this happen more often than you would care to believe! It's another reason for the equipment to be operated by the tech and only the tech!

To go back to the evolution of the equipment, the new cameras are much more user friendly. They are almost all plug and play type of equipment. You usually don't have to adjust aperture, or focus on a camera anymore. They come with auto-everything. Auto focus, automatic compensation for light levels and they have a higher resolution. They weigh ounces rather than pounds and can be carried between two fingers rather than two hands. They are durable and shock resistant.

Some of the pre-fabricated cameras are ready to install by just sticking them on a wall. In some ways, it takes away the art of hiding a video camera.

Some cameras have a miniature transmitter incorporated. They can transmit short distances, thus eliminating the need for wires between the camera and the recorder.

Most video cameras are also sensitive to IR, or infra-red light. IR can be used to illuminate an area for a camera and still appear to be dark to the human eye. It works like the night vision equipment, only better.

(Video Kit)

(Pen Cameras)

These tiny cameras are being used everywhere for all kinds of applications. There is a new diagnostic pill used by doctors to diagnose gastro-intestinal problems in their patients. This "pill" is a tiny camera, light and transmitter built into a capsule that can be swallowed by the patient. The camera takes pictures inside the body and transmits them to a receiver worn on the belt.

After the pill is ingested, the patient can go about his normal activity while the camera is taking pictures on it's trip through his digestive tract. These pictures are then downloaded and used by the doctors to pinpoint problems that they would otherwise need to perform surgery to observe.

(Given Diagnostic M2A "Pill" Camera)

Surveillance Vans

Most law-enforcement departments have some kind of vehicle, usually a van, set up for surveillance. A lot of these are crude and can be spotted a mile away by those looking for them.

I remember working a case with a local police department that needed my services to install some video equipment. When I arrived at the office, the shift captain informed me that the officer I would be working with was on a stake out.

He offered to drive me to the stake out and meet with that officer. As we arrived on the scene, which was a small medical clinic, I noticed a black van, with dark windows parked in a corner of the lot. The clinic had been the target of break-ins by perps looking for drugs.

A cloud of smoke was coming out of the ceiling vent of the van. There were four police officers in the van watching the clinic. They were all heavy cigarette smokers, hence the smoke! This was the only vehicle in the lot and might as well had "COP" painted on the side. I doubt seriously if anything ever came of the stake out.

(Typical Surveillance Vans)

Surveillance vans have come a long way from the old standard. Now there are all types of vehicles that are set up for video surveillance.

One of my favorites was a topper that slid into a pickup truck. A cord plugs into the cigarette lighter and powers the entire unit.

It is designed to fit into several different model pickups. You could use a blue Ford in the morning, and switch to a red Dodge in the evening. It works great in most Midwest environments where every other vehicle is a pickup truck.

There is enough room in the topper for one person to comfortably monitor the equipment, and there is a cover that you can slide over the bed to hide everything inside. The topper has a floor and is completely self contained, even to the extent of having a porta potty.

There are companies that make air-conditioning units for surveillance vans. These usually operate with dry ice and if you have ever been stuck in the back of a van in July on a stake out, you can appreciate one of these!

Vans are also equipped with some type of cooler for drinks and a desk of sorts with the surveillance equipment and a two way radio. All of the equipment is in the back of the van with a partition between the drivers' area and the back. There will be a door in the partition for access both ways.

(Interior of Surveillance Van)

I was on a stake out once where we were preparing to execute a no-knock search warrant after a controlled delivery. A no-knock means just that, you don't have to knock and announce your presence; you just kick in the door.

I was situated in the surveillance van on the street about a hundred yards from the target's house.

A controlled delivery is where an officer delivers a parcel that has already been searched and is known to contain drugs. The officer will be dressed in a postal uniform and driving a vehicle on loan from the local post office. Usually this officer is a postal inspector.

After the controlled delivery, the officer delivering the package is given time to clear the area, by which time the parcel is supposed to be opened by the addressee. Then the no-knock warrant is executed, by as many officers as are needed to enter all of the doors, generally by opening them with a battering ram, and arresting everyone in sight, hopefully before they can flush the drugs down the stool!

On this particular day, I had been sitting in the van for a couple of hours, waiting for everyone to get into position. I had a video camera focused on the front of the house, watching and recording the activity.

There were a bunch of kids, between ten and twelve years old going in and out of the house continually, before, during and after the delivery.

I was trying to keep an eye on them, when I noticed two men outside of the van I was occupying, giving it a looking over. This particular van was a conversion van that looked pretty fancy from the outside. The cab of the van was fairly plush with captains' chairs and a good stereo system.

The area all of this was going down wouldn't be considered the best part of town so I was a little concerned that maybe they were thinking about how much they could get for the van, or at least the wheels off of it.

I didn't want to be occupying the van if any of that took place, so I got on the radio and called for a black and white to make a slow pass by me, and when they did, the two men disappeared, like smoke!

In the meanwhile, these kids kept going in and out of the house after the delivery. This was on a school day, and there was no logical reason why these kids weren't in school.

I didn't know what the hold up was on the no-knock, but I got back on the radio and relayed the message that there wouldn't be anything to confiscate if they didn't get on the stick.

Sure enough, the team hit the house shortly after but came up empty handed. In the time it took them to crash the doors the package had been emptied and the goods were on the street.

The kids were their runners.

***

We built a number of vehicles we called "buy cars". They were used by the undercover officers to record buys of drugs or stolen merchandise. We installed one of the small CCD cameras in the steering column that would give a good view of the passenger side of the vehicle.

The car was also wired with a number of microphones to record conversations. The camera and the microphones were connected to a recorder and transmitter that were hidden in a false compartment in the trunk of the vehicle. The recorder would keep a record of what went on in the vehicle and the transmitter would send both video and audio to a back-up vehicle.

The idea was to record illegal transactions on the street. The buyers felt they were more secure in a car than they were out on the street or in an office.

An undercover Postal Inspector in Chicago used one of these vehicles with this equipment. On one of the first trips, a disgruntled postal employee was attempting to sell some checks he had stolen from the mail. As this was more or less a training trip, several back-up vehicles had tagged along for the ride.

They sat in the car negotiating the buy. The back-up vehicles were parked down the block. Suddenly, the buyer decided he wanted both the checks and any money the seller had. He pulled a revolver and said, "Give me the money, bitch!"

All of this activity was being recorded and transmitted. The inspector was very cool and played along with the buyer. He told him to point the gun elsewhere, he didn't want to get shot by accident.

The buyer, thinking he was a pretty tough operator finally wound up pointing the gun at the inspector with the gun behind his own arm. He would have had to shoot through his own arm to hit the inspector.

About this time, the car was surrounded by all the backups with their guns drawn.

The buyers only comment was, "Oh, Shit!"

It was a great tape and I'm sure it's still making the rounds.

(The night after I wrote this, I was watching "The Wildest Police Videos" on TV. Sure enough, there was the video of the buy car in Chicago!)

Wall Clock Camera

Wall Clock cameras are available through several commercial outlets. The camera used is a solid state CCD (Charge Coupled Device) with a pinhole lens that looks through a very small hole in the clock face that is virtually invisible.

A problem with the commercial version is that most do not come with audio capability. As many of them state, "Due to legal restrictions, our cameras are NOT equipped with audio.

Spy cameras with audio are illegal for public use and are reserved for law enforcement use only." This goes back to the 1968 privacy act. Video intercepts are O.K., but audio intercepts are not allowed under this act.

Go figure! Lip readers have been used in some cases. Many federal agencies still don't allow audio because the state codes aren't uniform and they don't want the hassle.

Connecting a radio shack microphone element to an audio input on the transmitter can still do it. You might get an echo effect to some degree, but will most likely be usable audio. I know this works because I have done it.

(Actual Wall Clock Cameras)

Wall clocks cameras are good because they give a better field of view than most other cameras. This is largely due to the fact that clock outlets that are installed in a lot of rooms such as offices, or kitchens and are placed so that the clock can be viewed from anywhere in the room. Conversely, the view back from the clock covers most of the room also. It makes for a quick and easy install.

Another reason for using a wall clock camera is getting power to it. Most clocks are plugged into an outlet. This is great for a camera install because you don't have to rely on batteries. The camera can be installed and run for years if you so desire.

Transmitters take a lot of juice even though cameras don't so unless you're hard-wired to a recording device you will be limited as to battery operating time for the transmitter. Also, if you're hard-wired, there goes the easy, quick install. You need the transmitter.

If you need the transmitter, you also need a receiver. Most of the transmitters in these cameras operate at a frequency of 2.4 Ghz. or higher. This is good! At that frequency, up in the microwave range, the signal will penetrate most common construction materials easily.

You can get a range of up to ½ mile with a 1-watt transmitter. Leafy trees and vegetation will kill the signal, however, so you need to avoid placing your equipment with this type of vegetation in the signal path.

Ideally, you can set your receiver up in a vacant room, a parked vehicle, or even above the ceiling tile in an adjacent building.

As a side note, these microwave transmitters will trigger a car-mounted "Fuzz Buster". They operate in the same range as a radar gun used by the traffic cops. I have used a fuzz buster to do a drive by check on a transmitter.

You can take the signal from the receiver and plug it into a time-lapse video recorder or a computer with a video card so you can record in digital. The signal from the camera will be transmitted 24/7 so the only restriction is on the recorder and the record mode.

The old recorders used a standard T-120 VHS tape. You have an option of using a thinner mylar tape that will record 160 minutes (T-160) which in the time lapse mode will give you about 30% more record time (or about 30 hrs on the 24hr real time VHS recorders).

These recorders also had a built in time/date generator to display the time and date on the video. The tapes have to be played back on another of the same recorders, but that video can be copied to a standard recorder using a tape that would work in your home video system.

The only problem to that is that you can only record a maximum of 6 hours per tape for your home system. Usually, unless there is an awful lot of activity, you only need a few minutes of real time to record any criminal activity for playback.

So there you are! All you have to do is walk into the target area, plug in the clock and walk out. The rest of your activity will be outside of the target area. Once you have the receiver and recorder set up and running in the mode you desire, you only have to check it once in awhile to replace a tape.

If you run into a lot of dead time, like when the lights are out and the room is vacant for a long period of time, you can use a motion sensor that operates on the receive end. It will activate the recorder when there is a change in the video, such as lights being turned on, or motion detected in the video signal. That will save a lot of tape during the inactive periods. This alarm function can be set for when to activate, what duration, etc., it is totally programmable.

After the case, if push comes to shove, you can just abandon the camera. In most cases, no one will ever know it's there. They are cheap enough to throw away and most of the commercial clock cameras are constructed so you can't tell what their primary purpose is.

Motion Sensor Cameras

Motion Sensor Cameras are probably a second choice to the Wall Clock Camera. They come in both wireless and hard-wired versions. They work well for the same reason as the clock camera; they have a good field of view. If it is used in the wireless version, its use is restricted to the battery life.

They work well when the motion sensor controls the operation of the transmitter and video. If they are in a high traffic area, however, they will soon run down the battery unless they are hard wired.

They are usually installed in the hard-wired version in order to utilize the multi functions to their greatest advantage and to increase the install life without frequent visits to change the battery.

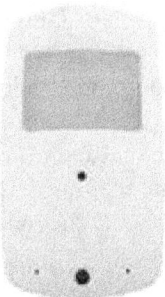

(Typical Motion Sensor Camera)

The best application for a writer to use in a story is to replace an existing motion sensor. The output of the motion sensor, which is nothing more than a switch, can be used to activate an alarm, or turn on or off a multitude of peripheral equipment.

The motion sensor is generally a passive infra red sensor. A passive infra red sensor is activated by motion and body heat. The motion sensor puts out a number of infra red beams, generally in a fan propagation. If a person walking through the room crosses the beams, the sensor is activated.

The range and sensitivity are adjustable. Infra red beams are invisible to the human eye. Contrary to movie and television scenarios, throwing a powder or blowing smoke into the room will not make the beams visible.

The video portion of the motion sensor camera is usually a solid state, CCD or CMOS in either a black and white or color configuration. They operate under extreme low light conditions and by using an infra red lamp, can operate very well in what appears as complete darkness to the human eye.

Motion sensors are very common in our surroundings anymore. That's why they would work well in a novel. In real life, bypassing an alarm or shutting off the alarm with the code would have no effect on the motion sensor camera. The camera would still function, and the motion sensor switch would still work.

That should be remembered when incorporating one of them into a work of fiction. They are generally attached to a wall with a mount that is screwed to the wall. The mount allows the camera/sensor to be positioned for the best coverage.

Most actual sensors have a tamper switch. The switch, when tripped, sends an alarm to a central monitoring point whether the alarm panel is activated at the pad or not. This should be remembered when replacing a sensor with a sensor-camera.

Tampers are usually activated when the sensor is opened up. They will also be activated if the wires are cut. For realism, the tamper switch should be taken into consideration.

To bypass a tamper, you should short the wires between the sensor and the panel, and cut the wires between the short and the sensor.

That about covers the Motion Sensor Camera. It would be a good choice if a Wall Clock Camera weren't practical.

There is one other system that uses motion to record video. It is called a Video Motion Detection System. This system detects movement in front of a fixed camera. Obviously, they cannot be used in a high traffic area. However, they are very useful to watch an area that is supposed to be secured, such as a locked room. They activate the recorder when a change in the video signal occurs.

Video Recording

Video cameras used for surveillance are usually watched live, but in order to capture that video, you must have a recorder of some type. Video recording and storage methods have changed enormously over the past decade. One of the first devices used for video recording was a reel to reel recorder using 1" videotape. Black and white mode only, of course, color video wasn't even in production then. The recorder was a foot thick, two feet wide and stood about five feet tall. It weighed something like one hundred pounds! This was supposedly for home recording but was priced out of the average homeowners' budget. Needless to say, this was not for covert operations. Now, recorders are small enough to be carried in a shirt pocket. Cameras are small enough to be hidden in a pair of glasses.

There are a lot of 8mm time lapse recorders available now also. They are much smaller in size that the old VHS type and some are built into small briefcases with a receiver, antenna and color monitor. Most of these can be powered either from a cigarette lighter plug in an automobile, or from a regular 110volt outlet. Some have their own rechargeable battery packs built in. A lot of the components are top end Sony and Hitachi. Companies that specialize in this type of equipment assemble them into the briefcase configuration.

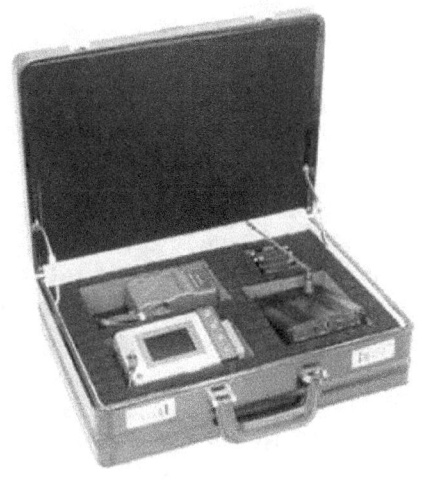

(Briefcase Video Setup)

(miniature recorder with LCD screen)

(Eyeglass camera)

Now, almost all video capture is done by digital recording. DVR's, digital video recorders, are faster, have more capacity, better resolution and are just better, period. Most of the old video recorders used by law enforcement agencies used video cassettes. Theses were the same cassettes that movies were recorded on and rented at your neighborhood video store to play on your VCR. By the way, VCR stands for Video Cassette Recorder. That includes any video recorder that uses tape on a cassette.

The recorders used by law enforcement were very different from your home VCR. They recorded in what was called "time lapse" mode, which is a method of recording events over a longer period of time, up to 960 hours on a standard video cassette. They could also record in a "one-shot" mode, which takes a snap shot or still picture either at a pre-determined interval, or when triggered by an outside device.

I once had to set up a time lapse recorder in the one-shot mode. There was someone using stolen credit cards to access automatic teller machines (ATM). They were withdrawing the maximum amount of cash from the cards. They had obtained the "PIN" (Personal Identification Numbers) for the cards. The PIN numbers were usually mailed in a separate envelope several days after the credit cards were mailed. This person knew what to look for and not only stole the credit cards, but the pin numbers too. They made a mistake by using the same ATM several times. I installed a hidden camera that was focused on the ATM. I set up the recorder in the "one-shot" mode. The recorder had an alarm input jack that could be used to activate the one-shot and take two or three still photos on the VHS tape. With the help of the bank employee that serviced the ATM, I connected the recorders alarm input jack to the contacts of the card reader in the ATM.

Using the one-shot mode, the tape would last about ninety days, depending upon the amount of ATM activity. Back then, It usually took about that long for the bank to determine that the card used to withdraw cash was a stolen card.

The ATM and the recorder were synchronized as to time and date, so when the card was identified, we searched the tape to that activation and "Bingo!", there was the thief! With the picture in hand, we got a confession and closed the case.

The alarm input on the VCR's was used quite a bit. I've connected door contacts, motion sensors, light switches, TV switches, and telephones to name a few. The main reason for using the alarm input was to save recording time on the tape. You don't want to review hours and hours of nothing on a tape.

Using the alarm input activates the recorder only when something happens that you want to see.

Video recording is becoming a very important tool in the security field. Facial Recognition is gaining acceptance and is being used for security screening at airports and many other targets of terrorism. The technology is rapidly approaching reliablity close to fingerprint identification.

(4 channel DVR)

Digital recording is coming into use, big time, especially for security systems. Digital video has many advantages over analog video, such as used in a VCR. One of the primary advantages is that it can be transmitted over telephone lines to a remote viewing and/or recording site. It can be stored as a file on a computer and transmitted via email, or through an FTP (File Transfer Protocol) site. Digital video can be recorded on thumb drives, digital tape, CD's, or computer hard drives. New methods and uses are being created all of the time.

Digital recording is coming into broader acceptance in the law enforcement community also. One of the reasons this has taken so long, was that digital video could be altered. A digital image can be captured on a computer and altered in any way you can imagine. Cut and paste and you can put anyone on the screen in the commission of whatever activity you have recorded.

Any tech can also tell you that he can take an analog image from a tape, import it as digital into a computer, do whatever to it, and then download it to an analog tape. The courts are beginning to believe that it is the testimony of the officer on the scene as to whether or not the video has been altered.

Pole Pig

It must have been a January, I remember it was bitter cold and I wasn't dressed for the weather. The two crew members were wearing insulated coveralls. I wore jeans and a leather jacket. I didn't have any gloves and my hands were stuffed into my jacket pockets. I had on a hard hat given to me by the power company security supervisor.

The idea was to make me blend in with the rest of the crew. I had to be there so that the two that were installing the pole pig would have it in the right location to view the activity at our target's location.

A pole pig is a remote controlled, high resolution camera that is mounted inside of one of those big round transformer cans you see on the power company poles. They have the big insulators on top that connect to the power lines. The real transformers are used to step down the voltage from the power lines to a level used by the households.

In our case, the can is a dummy filled with our equipment. It has a window made of one-way glass concealed on one side of the can that the camera looks through. They are powered by the regular power lines.

(Pole Pig)

The camera itself is a high resolution, low light video camera. It is controlled by a hand-held radio with a telephone type touchpad. By keying the radio and holding a certain buttons on the touchpad, you can tilt the camera up and down, or pan it from side to side. The buttons also control the lens by zooming in and out and controlling the focus. The camera is connected to a microwave transmitter that sends the signal to a remote location, sometimes called the "listening post", or LP.

The range of the microwave transmitter will be up to a mile or more, depending upon terrain. Trees will kill a microwave signal, especially in the spring and summer when the sap if flowing and the leaves are out. The radio that controls the system has a longer range. At the LP, the signal will be fed from a receiver to a recorder and monitor. Depending upon the activity, the action may be viewed and recorded live, or recorded in time-lapse mode for later viewing.

The Power Company mounts the pole pig to the pole. Some companies will charge for this service, but in this particular case, it was done as a courtesy. I had called and made arrangements with the head of security for a convenient time for both of us and now I was on site with the crew.

The pig weighs about fifty pounds and is lifted in place by the crane on the truck. The crew then fastens the pig to the pole and connects it to the electrical power. That is when I have to make sure it is positioned right so that it covers the area we want to watch. I do this by having a small monitor and microwave receiver with me in my van. I watch the monitor and use the radio to check for operation and location while the crew from the Power Company is still on site.

We had just finished connecting the pig when we ran into our first problem. The target was located in a shallow valley. The signal from the pole pig wouldn't reach our listening post, which was in one of our offices about a mile from the scene. We would either have to find another LP, or set up in a surveillance van. I came up with another option.

The radio signal, controlling the camera operation, would reach the pig from our LP. It was the microwave signal that carried the video from the pig to the LP that wasn't making the trip, due to the terrain. I found a church that was between the pig and the LP that was willing to let me set up a microwave transmitter and receiver in their attic. This acted as a repeater site. The receiver would pick up the signal from the pig and feed it to another transmitter that relayed the signal to our LP.

This turned out to work great. We set our monitor and recording equipment up in a vacant office and our LP was in business.

This microwave transmitter and receiver equipment is fairly expensive. At least on our budget it was. We had around $50,000 worth of equipment working on this case.

The idea behind using microwave is that it is at such a high frequency, that specialized equipment is needed to pick up the signal. At least, that is what was supposed to happen!

This was a pretty high profile case that involved the F.B.I., the I.R.S., the State Criminal Bureau of Investigation, the local PD, the county Sheriff and our own agency. It was our equipment that was being used, as none of the other agencies had anything like that available.

I was the tech assigned to get the equipment installed and working. We had information from a C.I. (confidential informant) that the target was involved in buying and selling stolen merchandise in a big way. It involved transporting stolen goods across state lines and an interstate fencing operation. Getting the goods on this guy could close a lot of cases for a lot of agencies.

At the LP, all of the equipment was working great. We had good visuals of everything that was going on. We monitored the coming and going of vehicles. We were even able to zoom in and get license plate info. We watched the unloading of merchandise into the large garage belonging to our target. We were ready to start taping and documenting the activity to get probable cause for a search warrant.

The following day, shortly after we were set up and before we were ready, everything stored at the suspects' garage was packed up and moved. No more vehicles came to unload. We couldn't figure out what had happened. Had he been tipped off?

We were in the dark until the Sheriff's office got a call from our target. He asked the sheriff why he was being watched and demanded that it stop. The sheriff sent a deputy to the house to handle the complaint. The deputy answered the call and went to the targets house. He, the deputy, reported to us later, that he could see everything we were watching on channel 73 of the target's television set. Not good!

We wound up taking the equipment down and the case went into limbo. Several months later, our suspect was robbed and shot. He was known to carry a bankroll of up to $20,000 on his person, and in his crowd, that was something that should have been kept a secret!

I never found out what happened to him after that. My part in the investigation ended when the equipment came down. After many phone calls, I finally met up with a representative from the company that made our expensive microwave equipment.

I had sent the equipment back to the company for testing. It seems our transmitter in the pole pig had developed a "leak". Instead of just transmitting on the safe microwave frequency, it was also transmitting on "harmonics". Harmonics are frequencies above and below the desired transmitting frequency. One of those frequencies matched up with the UHF band on channel 73. The harmonics transmitted far enough to be picked up on nearby television sets and far enough to blow our case.

I had used the pole pig many times before, and have many times since and this was the only time I ever had this problem with it or the microwave transmitters. It was also the only time I had that many people depending on the operation of it too.

The repeater idea worked great, and we've used that since. The pole pig was a great surveillance tool and has evolved into other conformations. There are still pole pigs in use, so next time you see a transformer hanging on a pole, give it another look, it just might be a pig!

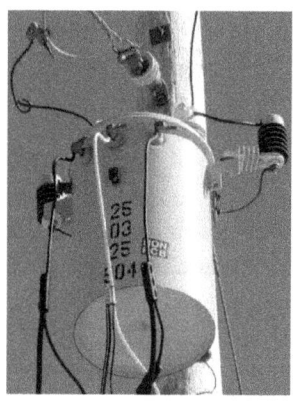

(Pole Pig?)

Installations Tips & Tricks

First thing to do is get an eyeball on the target area. It is extremely difficult to do an install cold. You have to know what you want to see from the camera's point of view.

Lighting is important. If at all possible, available light should be used. If the action takes place in the dark, you may need to install an infrared light. If you're not sure, put in the infrared.

If you use a single camera, the best bet is to get a view from above head height. The clock camera works well for this.

(Clock Cameras)

It is generally installed above eye level and has a field of view that covers a greater area. If at all possible, you need to get the placement of the camera to where you can see all of the activity in the room.

The Wall Clock Spy Camera would work well for this. The camera, microphone and transmitter are hidden behind the clock face. The clock is plugged into a regular AC outlet for power that runs all the separate components.

A lot of rooms, like kitchens and offices, have an outlet expressly for a clock. The outlet is recessed and has a hook for the clock to be hung on. Prefab camera units, such as the Wall Clock Camera are designed to be plugged in and left. Therefore, placement is critical. Once they are plugged into the outlet, they will run indefinitely, or until power to the unit is cut.

Depending upon the structural environment, the transmitter will send audio and video from 50 feet up to a half-mile. That is the tricky part, determining the range of the transmitter. The range can vary also, if there is pedestrian or vehicular traffic between the transmitter and receiver.

The 2.4 Ghz is up in the microwave range and will penetrate most structures, such as wood, brick, concrete, etc. The drawback to microwave is that trees will effectively ground out the signal. The signal will also "bounce", so placement of the receiver in relationship to the transmitter is also critical. Most receiving units have a signal strength meter that indicates whether or not you have sufficient signal for viewing and recording. If you have a good reading, you're in business.

I've used the above setup several times. When I first started using wall clocks, I had to build my own. In one case, I used the existing clock and added the camera and transmitter after hours and re-hung the camera in the same spot. It's much quicker and easier using the prefab clock cameras.

If you use an analog unit to record the video, like a VCR, you are restricted to recording time by the tape you use. Videotapes come in different recording lengths, such as T-120, T-160, etc. A T120 tape in SP mode of recording will give 2 hours of recording, real time. 4 hours at LP, real time, and 6 hours at EP, real time. Some special recorders will give up to

24 hours of real time recording on a standard T-120 tape. This means that if you want to record every minute around the clock, you need to change the tape once a day. If you set the record time from say, 8 a.m. until noon, and 1 p.m. until 5 p.m., you will be recording 8 hours a day and you only have to change the tape every three days. There are also recorders that are time lapse, which means you record in a slow mode for up to 960 hours on a standard T-120 tape. In this mode, you can also miss a lot of the action, as the camera isn't being recorded in a constant mode. Playback is jumpy also.

Using DVR, or digital, eliminates the old problems we had with VCR's.

Most professional recorders for law enforcement have an alarm input also. In this mode, an outside source, such as a door contact, motion detector, or similar source switches on the recorder. In the alarm mode, the recorder can record at whatever speed is programmed, for whatever duration you prescribe.

This is a very useful tool for a room that isn't occupied 24/7. The recorder can be programmed to record in real time for say, five minutes when the alarm is tripped. Depending upon what activity you are trying to capture, this method can work well for you.

Nearly all recorders of these types have a clock function that displays the time and date of the recording. They also allow input for a line of alpha characters to describe the site being recorded. It is important to set the clock with a reliable source that can be referred to in court, if it is needed. The recorders will adjust automatically for daylight time, so that needs to be noted also. Document everything; from start to finish, you never know when you'll need it!

If you are using digital, the options are much greater. The signal can be transmitted over telephone lines or fed into a web site for viewing anywhere in the world. The video and audio can be stored on a hard drive, a thumb drive, a DVD or CD, or in virtual memory. It can be downloaded to a standard VCR for recording on a VHS tape for playback. All or portions of it can be re-transmitted over the Internet.

You want to be sure you have a secure path so that you aren't transmitting to everybody on the internet and your video can't be intercepted. You don't want your case to show up on YouTube before you go to trial!

There is a digital camera with a built in chip that can record up to ninety minutes of digital video to the chip. The camera is powered by a small battery and can be reused.

Digital video is widely accepted by the security industry. It is much easier to work with, is cheaper and has less maintenance than the old analog systems. New technology such as Facial Recognition is totally digital. The applications for digital video are endless. If you are really interested in pursuing more information about it, I suggest you do a search on the Internet. Just enter "digital video" for search criteria and see what you get.

Once you know what you need to record, what equipment you will be using, where, when, what, how and why, you're ready to start. I always tried to have two of everything. Murphy's law will get you otherwise. I've had to make many trips to

Radio Shack on a last minute basis! I usually wear a vest, something like a fishing vest, with lots of pockets. I put all of my hand tools, connectors, batteries, solder and tape in the pockets.

I have a flashlight that is on a headband plus a small hand held flashlight. I would try to wear loose, comfortable clothes and tennis shoes or shoes with rubber soles, there is less chance of static electricity, and they are quieter. If needed, I would have a fake ID and uniform of a repairman, such as a telephone installer. I even had the hard hat for that one.

Before doing anything at the site, I would walk around taking Polaroid pictures. That way, I could refer to them after the install to be sure nothing had obviously changed.

I always tried to catch all of my wire clippings and strippings. I had a small vacuum that I would use to clean up any dust from cutting wallboard or ceiling tile.

If the area was already dusty and dirty, I tried to leave it as dirty as I found it. That was more difficult because I had to catch all of my dust and clippings instead of vacuuming them after.

Usually the installs were done in the middle of the night. Occasionally, they could be done in broad daylight, and once I did one right in front of the subject. He thought I was working for the power company.

Many of the installs are in motel rooms. Buys of stolen goods or drugs and meetings to set up buys are done many times in motels and hotels. Usually we worked with the hotel or motel management to do the installs. I did have one camera setup installed in a suitcase that the agent could just lay on the bed without any other devices being installed in the room. The suitcase had a false lining that hid all of the equipment.

Those are some of the installation tips. If you have a specific scenario that you have a problem with, send me an email and I'll see if I can get a solution for you. Good luck!

Common CCTV Terms:

AGC: (Automatic Gain Control) An electronic circuit that automatically adjusts the gain of a signal as a function of its input or other specified parameter.

B.L.C. (Back Light Compensation): Electronically compensates for high background lighting, giving detail to objects which normally would be silhouetted.

BNC: Connector for Video cable, commonly used in the industry.

CCD: Charged Coupled Device. A solid state semiconductor imaging device often referred to as an Integrated circuit, chip or "imager." Solid state cameras are often referred to as CCD cameras.

CCTV: It is the abbreviation for Closed Circuit Television which is a private or closed television system.

Coaxial Cable: A type of shielded cable capable of carrying a wide range of Frequencies (video or audio) with very low signal loss.

dB (Decibel): A logarithmic ratio of two signals or values, usually refers to power, but also voltage and current.

DSP (Digital Signal Processing): Refers to the electric circuit section of a device capable of processing digital signals.

E.I. (Electronic Iris): Electronic Iris shuttering is the ability of the camera to compensate for moderate light changes in indoor applications without the use of auto
iris lenses.

FIELD OF VEIW: The area that can be seen by the camera.

Ghz (GigaHertz): One billion cycles per second.

HAD (Hole Accumulated Device): A type of CCD sensor with a layer designed to reduce interference.

I.R. (Infra-Red): A light where the frequencies are lower than visible lights whereby the CCD camera can use it for a light source, but it can not be seen by human eye.

IRIS: The adjustable opening (mechanical diaphragm) through which light can pass and be regulated.

LAN: Local Area Network

LENS: A transparent optical component that converges light rays to form a two dimensional image of that object. It can be made of glass or plastic. The best lens is made of glass.

LUX: A unit measuring the intensity of light. A one foot-candle = 10 lux.

MANUAL IRIS LENS: A lens with a manual adjustment to set the iris opening (f-stop) in a fixed position. Generally used for fixed lighting applications.

MONITOR: Device that converts electronic signals into the video image that is generated by the camera and lens

MULTIPLEXER: It is a device that allows you to view up to 16 camera images on 1 monitor screen at same time or one at a time. Much superior to sequential switcher, it records all cameras at the same time by using frame and time technology.

PAN: Side-to-side movement of a camera on a horizontal axis.

PIP: Picture in picture.

QUAD: Device that allows one view of up to 4 camera images on 1 monitor screen at same time or one at a time.

RCA CONNECTOR: A video or audio connector most commonly used in plug and play video or audio equipment.

RADIO FREQUENCY (RF): Signals with a repetition rate above audible range, but below the frequencies associated with heat and light.

RESOLUTION: A measure of the ability of a camera or television system to reproduce detail. Typically refers to the number of picture elements that can be reproduced with good resolution.

SCANNER: A device that can pan only.

SWITCHERS: Alternates the displayed video image from one camera to the next. Cameras cannot be viewed at the same time.

TFT (Thin Film Transmitter): This technology is used mainly for manufacturing flat computer and video screens that are superior to LCD screens. Color quality, fast response time and resolution are excellent for video.

TILT: The up and down tilting movement of a camera.

TIME-LAPSE VCR: Video recorder that can record frames with pauses between them, thereby extending the time that a standard tape will last. The longest time-lapse VCR is 960 Hrs. However, digital recorders can last for a much longer period and with better resolution.

VARIFOCAL LENS: A lens with a variable focal length. May be used as a wide angle, standard, or telephoto lens.

WAN: Wide Area Network

PART II

Introduction to Weapons

You have to have weapons if you want to write a mystery, right? The most common, and the ones I'm covering are firearms. There is a wealth of information available about firearms, but there are still a lot of errors written into otherwise terrific mystery stories.

I've included some of the weapons I've encountered during my career, and some I haven't. I've had quite a bit of experience with handguns. I used to do my own modifications on my handguns and I reloaded about all of my ammunition. Ammo got expensive when I was shooting a lot. I've enjoyed doing target shooting and combat competition. It also helped with the confidence level when I had to carry as part of the job.

I'm not going into a great deal of detail here. If you have questions about a specific weapon, you can always contact me through my website, http://www.jerryhooten.com/

If I can't find the answer, my brother is a gunsmith and I can always call on him.

Weapons

Automatic Pistol

Firearms are probably the most abused tools in mystery writing. Here is some gun info for use in your story:

- Pistols are technically automatics, not revolvers. Clips and magazines are used in automatics, not revolvers. Speed loaders are for revolvers. It's o.k. to call a handgun an automatic, though actually they are semi-automatic rather than true automatics. A full automatic weapon is the machine gun. The difference is that a semi-automatic pistol requires a pull on the trigger each time the gun is fired. A *true* automatic fires until the trigger is released or the weapon runs out of ammunition, whichever comes first.

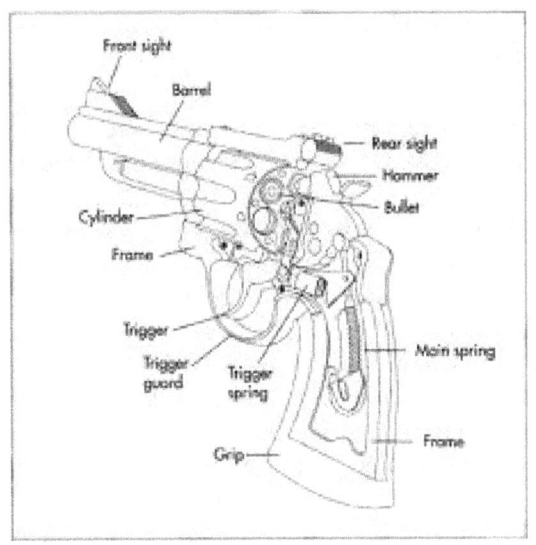

Labels in figure: Front sight, Barrel, Rear sight, Hammer, Bullet, Cylinder, Frame, Trigger, Trigger guard, Trigger spring, Main spring, Frame, Grip

<u>Revolver</u>

- Don't put silencers on revolvers. If you describe the weapon as something like, "A Colt Python", know what that means. A Colt Python is a revolver. Silencers do not work well on revolvers. They require a special shroud that covers the cylinder as well.
- Don't "put the safety on" on a revolver. Modern revolvers have a built in safety that doesn't allow the firing pin to come in contact with the cartridge unless the trigger is pulled all the way to the rear. (Old, *old* revolvers were carried with an empty chamber under the hammer. This was because the firing pin was part of the hammer and would rest directly on the

cartridge.) There is no button or lever to activate a safety on a revolver. The only manual safety function is a half-cocked position of the hammer on some revolvers.

- Most modern revolvers and pistols are "double-action". Double-action handguns are operated by pulling the trigger. This cocks the hammer and then releases it at the end of the trigger pull. Single-action weapons require cocking the hammer manually, usually with the thumb before pulling the trigger. The old "Colt .45 Peacemaker" used in western movies and the Colt Army Automatic are considered single action handguns. The Colt Army Automatic was cocked by pulling back the slide and releasing it. This would cock the hammer and chamber a round from the magazine. Most, not all, double-action *revolvers* are also capable of being fired single-action. Shooting a revolver single-action is usually more accurate than double-action as it requires a lighter trigger pull for a shorter distance. Single action *automatics* only require the first round to be chambered by cycling the slide. The recoil from firing the first round loads and cocks the weapon for the next shot. The usual method of carrying the single action automatic pistol is "cocked and locked", which means the slide has been cycled and a round is loaded in the chamber. The hammer is cocked, and the thumb safety is "locked" in the safe position. Double action automatics are carried with a round in the chamber and the safety on. Department rules may vary on the accepted method of carrying an automatic.

- Don't have a police officer use some exotic caliber for his side arm. Departmental rules are pretty strict on what the accepted ammunition is. Some common calibers for police departments are 9mm and .38 Special. If you describe a certain caliber, make sure the weapon you describe is actually made in that caliber. Generally revolvers use the .38 Special, Automatics use the 9mm. Lately, the new standard has become the .40 Caliber.
- Some weapons have individual characteristics.. The old Army Colt .45 Automatic is essentially for right-handed shooters. The magazine release, the thumb safety and the slide lock are all located on the left side of the pistol and are virtually impossible to readily access with the left hand. There are a lot of automatic pistols designed like the Colt Army Auto. If your hero is left handed, give him a Glock, a Smith & Wesson, or one of the newer military autos that are designed to be fired with either hand.
- Don't write in the weapon without doing a little research. Ask someone that knows his guns. It really adds to the story.

Beretta Model 93 - Shoots 3 shot bursts

SILENCERS:

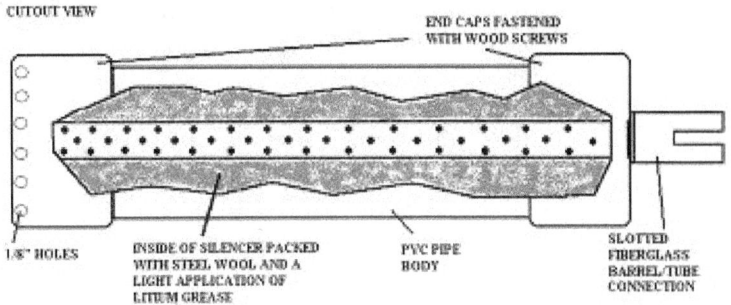

CUTOUT VIEW

END CAPS FASTENED
WITH WOOD SCREWS

1/8" HOLES

INSIDE OF SILENCER PACKED
WITH STEEL WOOL AND A
LIGHT APPLICATION OF
LITIUM GREASE

PVC PIPE
BODY

SLOTTED
FIBERGLASS
BARREL/TUBE
CONNECTION

Silencers are sometimes referred to as sound suppressors. They are illegal for private citizens to own or possess under federal firearms laws. They are usually constructed by inserting cylinders with perforations inside of other cylinders with packing in between the walls. The expanding gas emerging from the barrel of the gun is re-routed through the cylinders much in the same manner as exhaust gases from an automobile. A silencer is usually made for a specific weapon that has been modified to receive it. Although made for automatic or semi-automatic weapons, the efficiency of the silencer is increased by having the breach, or slide of the weapon locked closed so that escaping gases, or noise, is directed through the silencer itself. This disables the "automatic" function of ejecting the spent cartridge. The breach must be unlocked and manually cycled to eject the old cartridge and load the next round into the chamber. If the automatic function is required, the silencer becomes more of a "sound suppressor" than a true silencer. Bolt-action rifles, which eject and load rounds manually, work well with silencers. Especially when used with a sub-sonic round, such as a .22 or a hand loaded cartridge designed for sub sonic use. Sticking an orange or grapefruit on the end of the rifle, though not really very effective, can make a one-time silencer. The fruit absorbs some of the escaping gases and reduces the noise. It works better in books than real life.

SPECIAL WEAPONS:

Sawed off shotguns are popular in detective novels. A sawed off shotgun is illegal if the barrel muzzle to breach is less than 18" in length. The advantage of the short barrel is that the shot pattern is wider when the barrel is shorter and there is no "choke" on the barrel. A choke is a design feature that helps control the shot pattern for specific use. A full choke shotgun has the tightest pattern. It also has the greatest effective range. Shotguns with less choke and/or shorter barrels have a much shorter effective range, the shot disperses to the point where it is impractical as a weapon. The sawed off is great for very close work only.

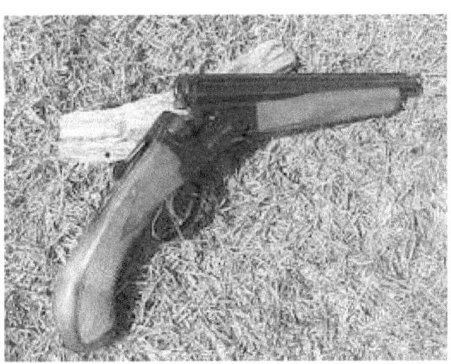

(A SBS - Short Barreled Shotgun - The Bearclaw)

Pump action shotguns still remain a favorite riot gun of many police officers. They have a lot of firepower with the seven round magazines. Usually, they are loaded with 00 buck, #4 shot, or birdshot, or a combination of the three. The most lethal of course is the double ought buck.

For years, the Model 97 Winchester pump was used by many law enforcement agencies.dd It was also used in the trenches in WWI.

 It had the nickname of "Crowd Pleaser" due to it's distinctive "Chunk, Clack" sound it made when chambering a round. It definitely got the attention of anyone on the receiving end!

<u>Winchester 97</u>

Another nickname, which is actually a model description, is the "Street Sweeper". It is a 12 gauge semi-automatic shotgun with a drum magazine, similar to the old Thompson sub-machine gun.

Due to the variety of loads available, such as rubber pellets, tear gas, etc., this is a valuable tool for any police department.

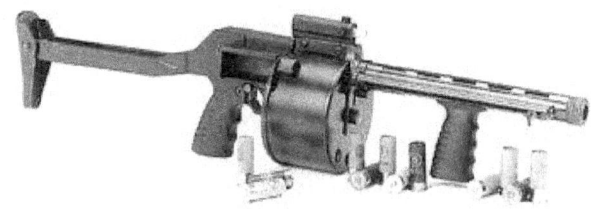

The Street Sweeper

Thompson

I had an opportunity to fire the Thompson .45 Caliber Sub Machine Gun. Quite an experience! Since it was a full automatic weapon, it would continue to fire as long as you held the trigger back.

Quite a bit of recoil using a full load .45! Rockola, the same company that makes jukeboxes, made the particular model I got to shoot. Remington and Colt, among others, also made them. It was a WWII model that had been confiscated shortly after the war from a slightly inebriated ex-G.I. who was trying to shoot beer cans floating in a river. I assume he "liberated" it. The Thompson was a favorite during prohibition days and got the nickname, "The Chicago Typewriter".

I saw an interesting adaptation of the shotgun while attending a training class at one of the academies. The shotgun shell had been opened up, and the shot removed from the case. In its place, a vial, filled with water and sealed, was inserted in the shell.

It was claimed that a shotgun using this load could be used to open a locked door when executing a "No Knock" search warrant. Firing the shotgun with the end of the barrel directly against the door, the water, which will not compress, would take out the door, and if the door had a very good multiple locking systems, the entire doorframe would be blown out. I never got to see this in practice, but some of the officers attending the class swore to it.

The Heckler and Koch MP-5 submachine gun is used by many law-enforcement agencies. It uses a 9mm bullet and has a high rate of fire when used in the full auto mode. It has a collapsible stock that when in, gives the MP-5 an overall length of only 21 inches. Fully extended, it is 27 ¼ inches long. It weighs only 6 ½ pounds.

H&K MP-5

COLLATERAL DAMAGE:

Don't forget that using a weapon often has collateral damage. Innocent bystanders can and do receive injuries in a shoot out. The 9mm round, which is becoming a standard police caliber, has great penetration capability, especially when used with the solid bullet. It will penetrate an entire vehicle, several interior walls of a building, or several human bodies. The hollow point bullet expands upon contact and imparts greater energy and damage to the target. It also has fewer tendencies to penetrate walls.

NIGHT VISION:

There are some excellent night vision scopes available for weapons on the market. Some use infra-red technology, some use light intensifiers, such as the starlight scopes, and some use thermal imaging. A lot of the night vision equipment is available to the general public now. Thermal imaging is a newer technology that uses the differences in temperature to define a target. The army has adopted it as standard issue for the new "Land Warrior" concept of foot soldier. Thermal Imaging is even used to find buried bodies that give off heat when decomposing. It has been used primarily by the military and is still cost prohibitive for most law enforcement agencies. It is capable of locating an enemy hiding behind a wall, and since most military small arms will penetrate a wall, it becomes very effective in eliminating those targets.

Thermal imaging has also posed some legal problems when used by law enforcement agencies to determine whether a house is occupied. There are arguments that it violates privacy laws. It will be a tool of the future, for sure!

<u>Night Vision Monocular</u>

Common Terms

ACP - Designation for a cartridge originally designed for an Automatic Colt Pistol (ACP)

BARREL RIB - Additional material along the top of the barrel that allows for quicker alignment of the muzzle with the target and adds weight to improve the balance of the firearm.

CALIBER - Used to identify appropriate ammunition for a firearm.

CAPACITY - Number of cartridges a firearm will hold.

CYLINDER - Part of a revolver, immediately behind the barrel, that revolves and has a number of chambers into which cartridges are placed.

DOUBLE-ACTION - Pulling the trigger both cocks the hammer and releases it to discharge a firearm. In double-action revolvers, pulling the trigger also revolves the cylinder.

ENHANCED MODEL - A firearm that has features not found on earlier models. Such features may enhance function, accuracy convenience use, or appearance.

FINISH - The outward appearance of the firearm that varies depending on the type of material, level of polishing, and chemical finish.

LIGHTWEIGHT (L.W.) - A firearm that is constructed of lightweight material such as aluminum alloy in the receiver or frame.

LOCKED BREECH - A feature of some firearms in which the barrel and breech mechanism are mechanically locked together at the moment of firing, which reduces recoil.

LONG COLT (.45) - A modern term used to identify the .45 Colt cartridges originally designed for the Colt Single Action Army revolver.

MAGAZINE - Removable part of pistols and rifles used to store and feed ammunition.

PISTOL - A hand-held firearm in which the ammunition is chambered in the breech of the barrel.

RECOIL - The movement of the firearm in the opposite direction to that of the bullet at the moment of discharge. In other words, the kickback of a gun caused by firing of the bullet.

REVOLVER - A firearm with a revolving cylinder in which there are a number of chambers that bring successive cartridges into line with the barrel each time the hammer is cocked (single action) or the trigger is pulled (double action).

RIFLING - Grooves in the bore of the barrel that impart spin to the bullet to improve its stability during its trajectory.

RIFLING TWIST - The rate the rifling in the barrel twists through 360 degrees and is expressed in "turns per inch."

SAFETY - A device designed to prevent discharge of a firearm until discharge is intended.

SEMIAUTOMATIC - A firearm that fires one round, extracts and ejects the spent cartridge case in recoil, then feeds another round from the magazine into the chamber each time the trigger is pulled.

SHORT-BARRELED RIFLE – An illegal rifle having one or more barrels less than sixteen inches in length and any weapon made from a rifle if such weapon, as modified, has an overall length of less than twenty-six inches.

SHORT-BARRELED SHOTGUN – An illegal shotgun having one or more barrels less than eighteen inches in length and any weapon made from a shotgun if such a weapon as modified has an overall length of less than twenty-six inches.

SIGHTS - Front and rear components used to align a firearm with its intended target.

SIGHT RADIUS - The distance between the sighting point on the rear sight and the sighting point on the front sight.

SINGLE ACTION - A firearm that requires the hammer or striker to be cocked manually before pulling the trigger to fire it. On revolvers, this is done by pulling the hammer back to the cocked position. On single action pistols, pulling the slide to the rear initially cocks the hammer. The firing of the pistol, with the resulting cycling of the action, cocks the hammer for each successive shot.

TRIGGER - The part of the action moved by the finger to fire the weapon.

VENTILATED RIB -A specialized barrel rib with cutouts that help to dissipate heat from the barrel and cut down heat shimmer along the sighting plane.

Part III Forms

Search and Seizure Warrant

Search Warrant, in law, written order by an official of a court authorizing an officer to search in a specified place for specified objects and to seize them if found. The objects sought may be stolen goods or physical evidences of the commission of crime (e.g., narcotics).

The Fourth Amendment to the U.S. Constitution, which protects against unreasonable searches and seizures, provides, in effect, that a search warrant may be issued only on oath or affirmation that a crime was probably committed.

In Mapp v. Ohio (1961) the U.S. Supreme Court mandated states to exclude from trial evidence obtained in illegal searches, such as those without a proper warrant. This "exclusionary rule" has been the subject of great controversy and subsequent litigation. In recent years, the Supreme Court has narrowed the scope of the rule, in many circumstances permitting the introduction of any evidence gathered in "good faith.

Courts have ruled that a wiretap constitutes a search that requires a warrant. Warrants are not required for the gathering of evidence in some circumstances. These exceptions include evidence gathered after a lawful arrest, inspections by customs or border officials, searches made with the suspect's consent, searches of items in plain view, and searches of the belongings of secondary students on school property.

Information on search warrants is easily available on the internet. State warrants, federal warrants, exclusions and exceptions are cussed and discussed ad naseum!

The use of a warrant in your book should reflect the area and department or agencies involved. Types and places of search need to be examined. A computer search would be different from a residence, or business, or auto, and all instances need to be looked at. The more realistic it is the better.

Another detail that isn't always covered in books and movies is the documentation that goes along with a search. You need an inventory, and to really CYA, a video of the actual search. Pictures tell a story. If you're executing a warrant, you want all the backup data you can get!

The following samples are just that, samples of what the actual documents would look like.

Sample Search & Seizure Warrant

AO 93 (Rev. 12/09) Search and Seizure Warrant

UNITED STATES DISTRICT COURT

for the

In the Matter of the Search of)
(Briefly describe the property to be searched)
or identify the person by name and address)) Case No.
)
)
)

SEARCH AND SEIZURE WARRANT

To: Any authorized law enforcement officer

An application by a federal law enforcement officer or an attorney for the government requests the search of the following person or property located in the _____ District of _____ *(identify the person or describe the property to be searched and give its location)*:

The person or property to be searched, described above, is believed to conceal *(identify the person or describe the property to be seized)*:

I find that the affidavit(s), or any recorded testimony, establish probable cause to search and seize the person or property.

YOU ARE COMMANDED to execute this warrant on or before _____
(not to exceed 14 days)

☐ in the daytime 6:00 a.m. to 10 p.m.   ☐ at any time in the day or night as I find reasonable cause has been established.

Unless delayed notice is authorized below, you must give a copy of the warrant and a receipt for the property taken to the person from whom, or from whose premises, the property was taken, or leave the copy and receipt at the place where the property was taken.

The officer executing this warrant, or an officer present during the execution of the warrant, must prepare an inventory as required by law and promptly return this warrant and inventory to United States Magistrate Judge

_____
(name)

☐ I find that immediate notification may have an adverse result listed in 18 U.S.C. § 2705 (except for delay of trial), and authorize the officer executing this warrant to delay notice to the person who, or whose property, will be searched or seized *(check the appropriate box)*   ☐ for _____ days *(not to exceed 30)*.
☐ until, the facts justifying, the later specific date of _____.

Date and time issued: _____   _____
Judge's signature

City and state: _____   _____
Printed name and title

Return		
Case No.:	Date and time warrant executed:	Copy of warrant and inventory left with:
Inventory made in the presence of :		
Inventory of the property taken and name of any person(s) seized:		

Certification

I declare under penalty of perjury that this inventory is correct and was returned along with the original warrant to the designated judge.

Date: _____

_____
Executing officer's signature

_____
Printed name and title

72

Consent to Search

•

Date: *(mm/dd/yyyy)*

I, , have been informed of and understand my constitutional rights not to have a search made of

without the requirement of a search warrant. I have also been informed of, and understand, my right to refuse to consent to the search. However, I hereby authorize *(Officer(s))*

to conduct a complete search of

located at

The *(Department or officers)* is/are authorized by me to take from the above described property any letters, papers, materials, or other property, which is contraband or evidence and specifically

I understand that this contraband or evidence may be used against me in court of law or an administrative proceeding.

I understand my right to withdraw my consent at any time.

This written permission is being given by me to the above named persons freely and voluntarily without threats, promises, or coercion of any kind to have me consent to the search and/or sign this form. I realize that I may ask for and receive a receipt for all things taken.

Signature of Witnesses: Signature of Consentor:

Search Warrant Inventory

Subject Name			Date (mm/dd/yyyy)		Position/Box :
Subject Address			Floor/Room No.		
Officer(s)			Case No.		
Safe	Cabinet	Credenza	Desk		Drawer
Shelf	Table	Wall	Other		

QUANTITY	

Page _____ of _____ pages.

What is a Subpoena?

A subpoena is a written court order requiring the attendance of the person named in the subpoena at a specified time and place for the purpose of being questioned under oath concerning a particular matter which is the subject of an investigation, proceeding, or lawsuit. A subpoena is issued by someone authorized by law, usually by the attorney for a party to a lawsuit, but very often issued by someone authorized to conduct an investigation such as the State Attorney General or local District Attorney.

In addition to requiring the attendance of a person, a subpoena may also require the production of a paper, document, or other object relevant to the particular investigation, proceeding, or lawsuit. Usually a subpoena directs that the person named appear and give testimony in open court. However, certain subpoenas require the person to appear before a person or tribunal other than a court, such as a grand jury.

A subpoena will identify the person who issued the subpoena as well as the general nature of the proceeding to which it relates, although not necessarily the precise subject matter of the proceeding. If you are served with a subpoena, you cannot ignore it. If you do, you risk being held in contempt of court, even if the subpoena was not signed by a judge.

When you are served with a subpoena, you must do one of two things. You must either comply with the subpoena or, if you have an objection, you must apply to the proper court for permission to vacate or modify the subpoena. Such an application would ordinarily require the services of an attorney.

In considering what to do if you are served with a subpoena, you should keep two things in mind. First, if you feel that you may be target of a criminal investigation or that your testimony may implicate you in criminal activity, however remote, you should immediately consult an attorney. Second, if there is any question in your mind about the validity of the subpoena, you should consider challenging the subpoena by applying to the proper court before you appear at the time and place designated by the subpoena.

If your only objection to the subpoena is that it may be difficult or impossible for you to appear at the time and place indicated, you should contact the attorney or person who issued the subpoena. Usually that person's name, address, and telephone number will appear at the bottom of the subpoena. It may be possible to postpone your appearance or to arrange a more convenient time for you to appear. If other arrangements cannot be made, or your appearance will jeopardize your health or your employment, you should seek the services of an attorney.

(Sample Subpoena)

REQUEST FOR GRAND JURY SUBPOENA

I request a grand jury subpoena <u>duces tecum</u>* to be issued for each of the persons or custodians of record listed below to appear before the United States Grand Jury, *** District of ****, for the month indicated, to present evidence concerning a suspected violation of Title ____, U.S.C.

§_____ or other law relating to

_____ in

[nature of offense]

<u>United States v.</u> .

[defendant(s) name(s)]

I have discussed this request with AUSA

_____, who has agreed it is necessary or desirable, will not jeopardize this or any other pending investigation, does not request privileged information and can be scheduled at that time. He/she has advised me of, and I understand, the secrecy requirements of Rule 6(e), Federal Rules of Criminal Procedure, concerning evidence obtained by a grand jury.

The requirements of this subpoena may be satisfied if the documents are turned over to me on or before the appearance date on the subpoena.** The documents requested are listed on the back of this page. The estimated number of pages of documents (if known) is _____ (only for reimbursement of financial institutions purposes).

I will be present to receive the subpoenaed documents and will immediately make and sign an inventory for the documents and provide a copy to the Assistant United States Attorney. I will also promptly fill out such other forms as may be required.

Dated: _____

_____

(Signature & Title of Requestor)

Print Name of Agent & Agency

Telephone Number of Agent

* Scratch <u>duces tecum</u> if documents are not subpoenaed.

** Scratch this sentence if prior turnover of documents not desired.

NAME, ADDRESS AND TITLE OF THOSE SUBPOENAED FOR MONTH OF
_____ :

_____ To be returned and served by requesting agent.

_____ To be served by certified mail by secretary.
#_____

Description of Documents Subpoenaed

Any and all records, correspondence, memoranda, messages, writings or other documents or information in computer or electronic (_e.g._, video or audio) or other form in your possession, custody or control, or which are available to you, relating to
_____ for the time period _____,
including but not limited to:

(Check applicable paragraphs and fill in blanks)

_____ 1. All bank statements, checks, deposit slips, account signature cards, drafts, withdrawal slips, notes, loan information, safe deposit box records, agreements or other records pertaining to the account or accounts, certificates of deposit, other assets or liabilities, or other transactions.

_____ 2. All telephone bills, pen registers, recordings or other records of telephone calls or telegrams to or from the telephone or address of

_____.

_____ 3. All bills, notes, contracts, agreements or correspondence of _____ with

_____.

_____ 4.

_____ 5. You are requested not to disclose the existence of this request to your {subscriber} {customer}. Any such disclosure could impede the investigation being conducted and thereby interfere with the enforcement of the law.

_____ 6. If you retain the original of these records, they are to be kept in your possession until notified they are no longer needed.

_____ 7. The requirements of this subpoena may be satisfied by your furnishing the requested information/documents to the _____ agent serving this subpoena.

NOTE: THE AUSA MUST BE ADVISED WHEN THE SUBPOENA IS SERVED.

The following shall be completed by the AUSA:

1. Advice of Rights Notice to be attached? Yes No

2. Non-Disclosure letter:

A. General? {SUBPOENA.LR1} Yes No

B. Penalty notice? {SUBPOENA.LR2} Yes No

C. Non-financial Institution {SUBPOENA.LR3} Yes No

3. Reimbursement paperwork? Yes No

(Obligation approved, OBD-211, Notice, Services Provided Form)

Subpoena Number: Approved by:

_____

_____

Assistant United States Attorney

Summary of my First Book

I intend to continue with these books. I still want to write something about Identity Theft, forgery and counterfeiting, lock picking and alarm systems. I think that would make interesting reading for mystery writers.

Please visit my website. www.jerryhooten.com. Send me an email if you have a question jerry@jerryhooten.com or I can do a manuscript review. Contact me for rates. My snail mail address is:

Jerry Hooten
PMB 101
2643 Beaver Avenue
Des Moines, IA 50310-3909

Let me know what you think of this book. I'd appreciate it!

Negative or Positive comments welcome!

Thanks,

Jerry